INCREDIBLE EARTH SCIENCE EXPERIMENTS FOR 6TH GRADERS

SCIENCE BOOK FOR ELEMENTARY SCHOOL

CHILDREN'S SCIENCE EDUCATION BOOKS

Speedy Publishing LLC

40 E. Main St. #1156

Newark, DE 19711

www.speedypublishing.com

Copyright 2017

In this book, we're going to talk about some Earth Science experiments you can do at home or at school. Make sure an adult is there to help you so you're safe when conducting experiments. So, let's get right to it!

WHAT IS EARTH SCIENCE?

Earth Science is a very large branch of science and encompasses many different categories. It includes:

- Geology, which is the study of rocks, minerals, and the processes that created them, like earthquakes and volcanoes.

GEOLOGIST IN CAVE

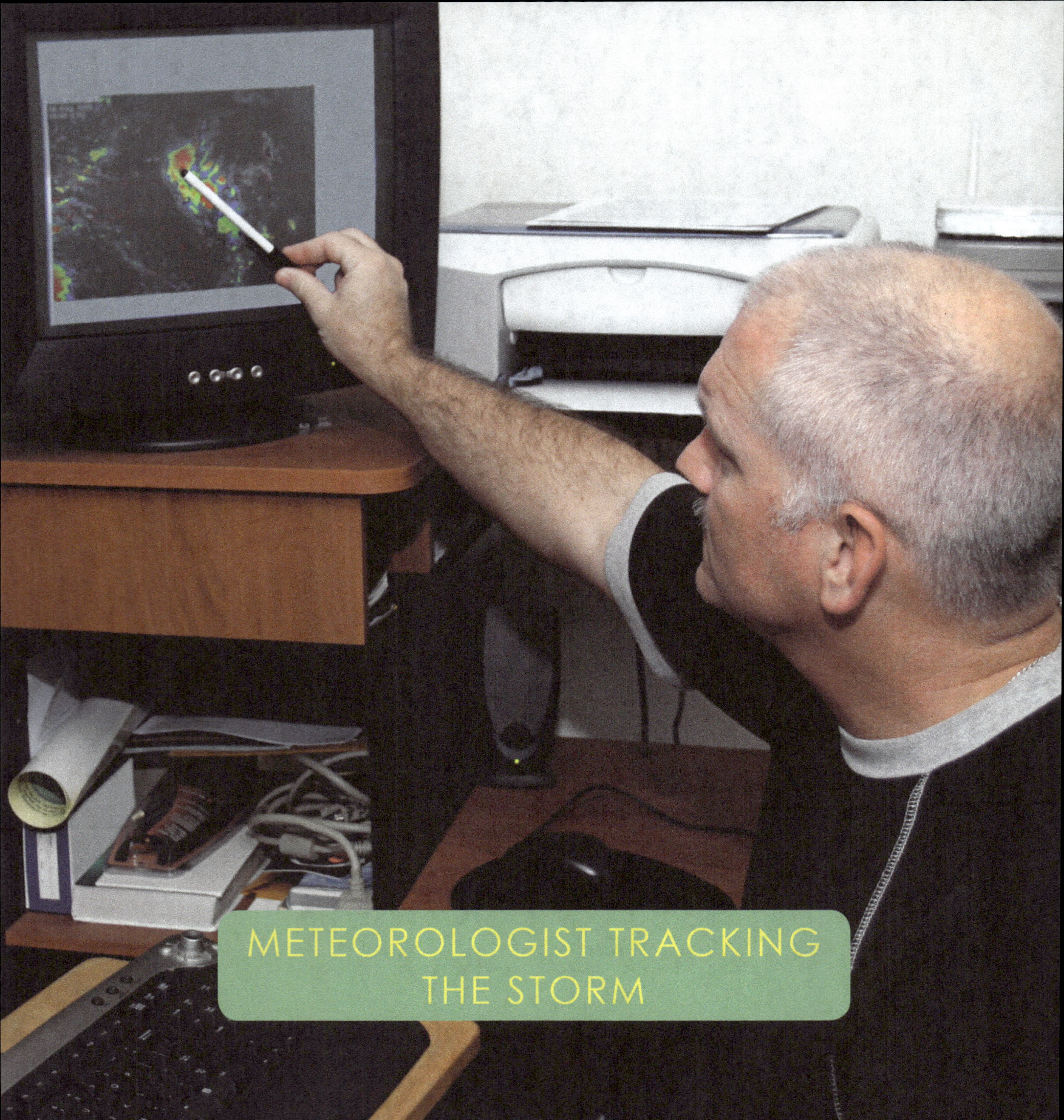

METEOROLOGIST TRACKING
THE STORM

- Oceanography, which is the study of everything related to the ocean

- Meteorology, which is the study of all different types of weather patterns that we have on Earth

- Climatology, which is the study of the trends of our entire atmosphere

- Environmental Science, which is the study of how human populations affect the Earth's environment

- Astronomy, which is the study of the celestial bodies in outer space

ASTRONOMER WITHIN AN OBSERVATORY

SEISMOLOGIST POINTING
AT THE EQUIPMENT

Most scientists who are interested in Earth Science specialize in a specific category or subcategory. For example, a scientist who is interested in geology might decide to become a seismologist.

A seismologist is a scientist who specializes in the study of the seismic waves caused by earthquakes. Seismologists do experiments to determine how seismic waves will impact areas of heavy population.

GEOLOGIST LOOKING AT
ROCK SAMPLE IN QUARRY

EXPERIMENT 1: THERE'S A WHOLE LOT OF SHAKING GOING ON

To do this seismology experiment, you'll need several items. You'll need a large pan made out of metal or plastic. If you use plastic, make sure it's a strong plastic. You'll need a few pounds of sand made up of fine grains. You'll also need water, a large serving spoon, and a table-tennis ball.

Last, you'll need a brick and a small rubber mallet. If you want to, you can use a power drill that operates with batteries. You'll need a PVC elbow or something similar if you decide to use the drill.

NEXT STEPS

Mix the sand with the water in the basin. Your layer of sand should be several inches thick and there should be adequate water soaking through. Combine it thoroughly and make sure that all the areas of sand are damp. There should be no water puddles.

On the right side of the pan, scoop out a deep hole and then bury the table-tennis ball there. We're going to pretend that the ball is a storage tank that's underground. Completely cover your "storage tank" with sand and smooth the sand on top so the "tank" isn't visible.

On the left side of the pan, push the skinny side of the brick down into the sand. This brick is going to be our "office building."

If you want to, spread some sand that's dry over the entire ground surface. Now it looks like our building is standing in dry ground.

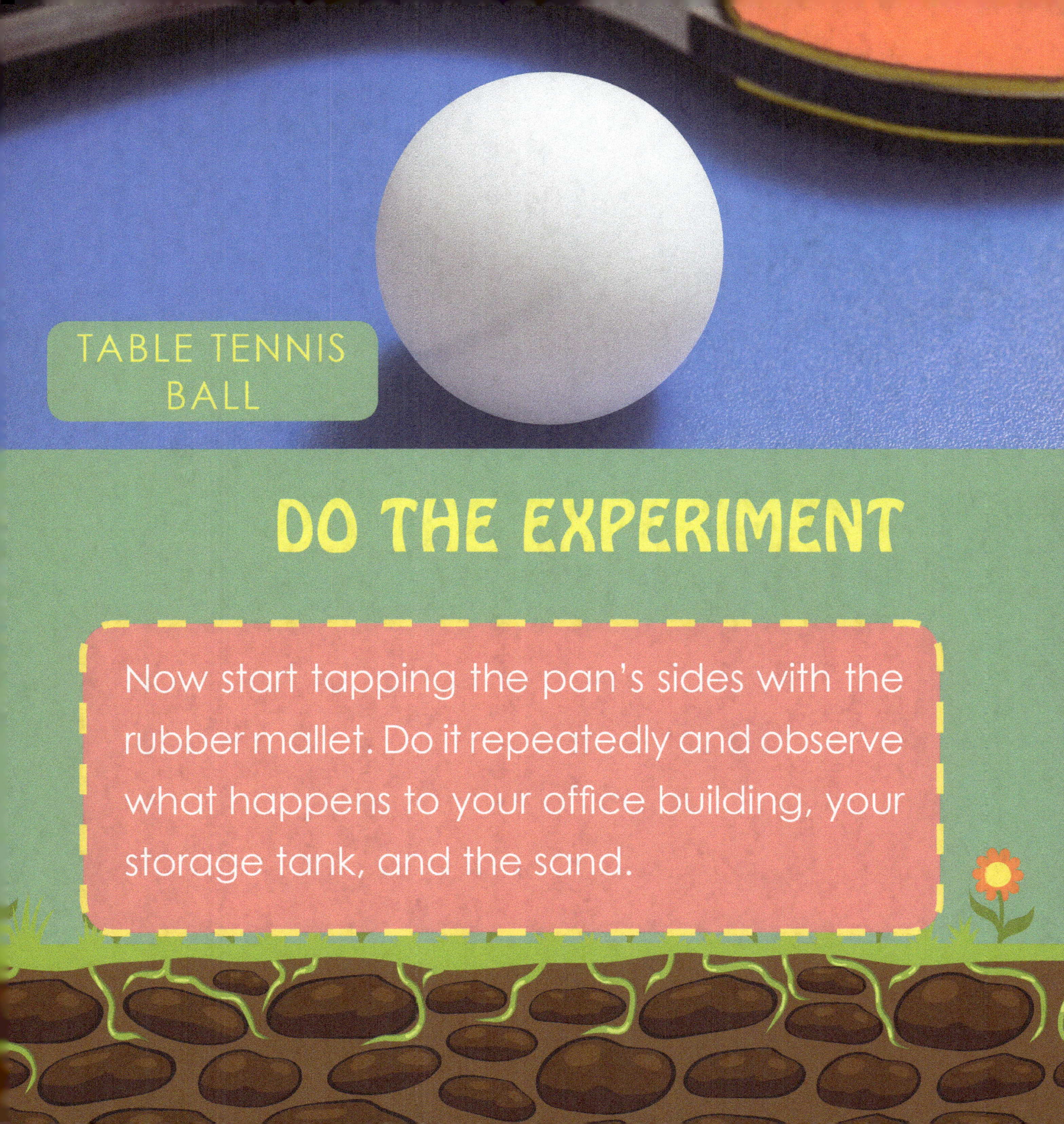

DO THE EXPERIMENT

Now start tapping the pan's sides with the rubber mallet. Do it repeatedly and observe what happens to your office building, your storage tank, and the sand.

If you want to use the power drill, attach a PVC elbow to its chuck, which is the clamp that usually holds the drill bits, so the drill will vibrate. Make sure it's on there tight and won't fall off. Then, push the drill's battery pack on the side of the pan. This will simulate an earthquake's shaking at a higher level of

frequency than you can do with the rubber mallet.

You may want to try the vibration from different corners of the pan. To "reset" the experiment, you can stir the compacted sand with the spoon to loosen it up again and reposition your building and storage tank.

SCIENTIFIC EXPLANATION

As you were shaking up the pan, you're simulating what happens when there's an earthquake. What happened to your office building? Did it shake a lot? Did it crash down to the ground?

What about your underground storage tank? Did it stay underground or did it rise to the surface? What happened to the sand? Was it flowing more like a liquid instead of moving like a solid?

RUINED BUILDING

FORMWORK FOR A CONCRETE
FOUNDATION, BUILDING SITE

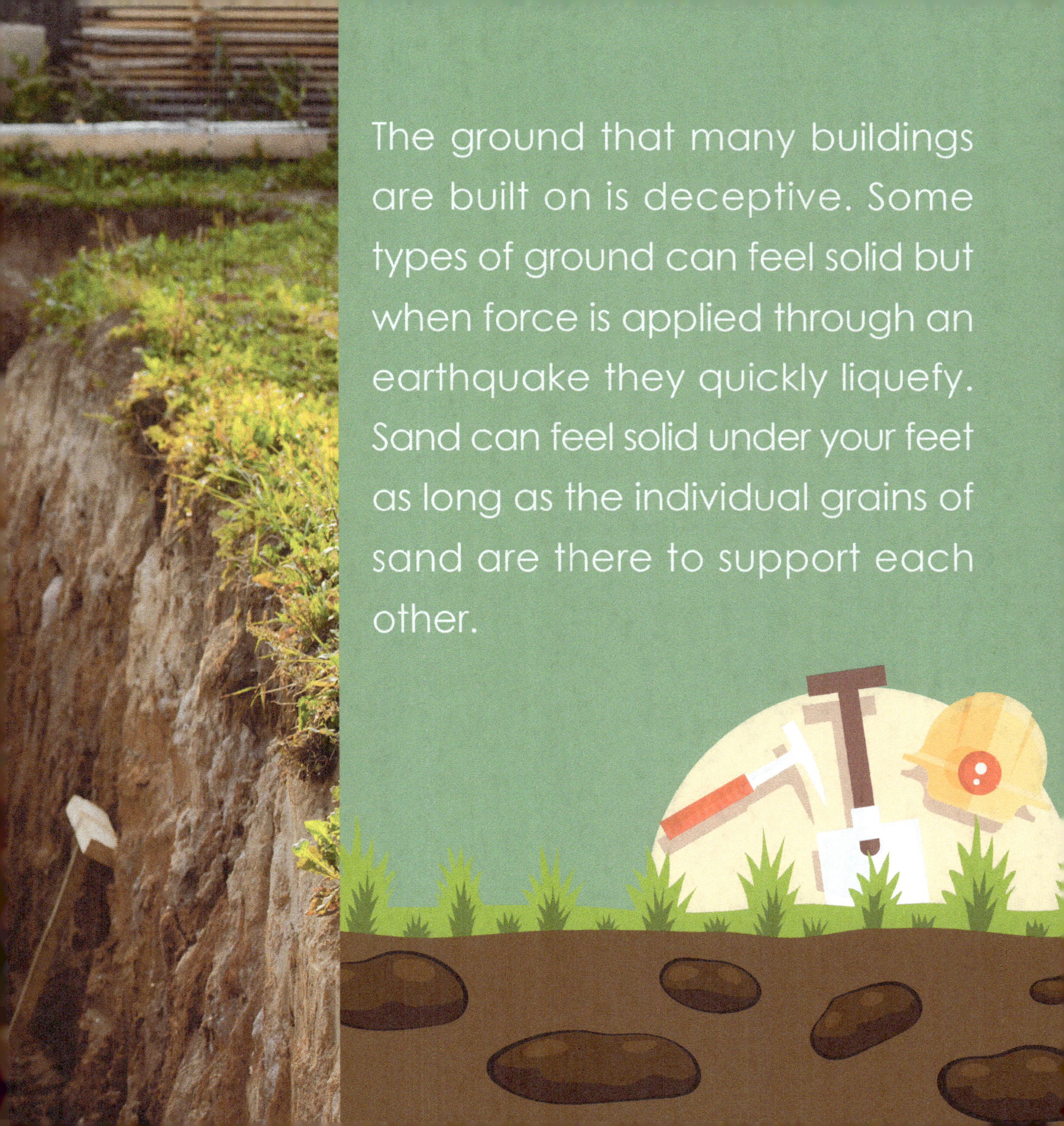

The ground that many buildings are built on is deceptive. Some types of ground can feel solid but when force is applied through an earthquake they quickly liquefy. Sand can feel solid under your feet as long as the individual grains of sand are there to support each other.

However, between the grains of sand there are empty spaces called pores. The so-called solid ground under your feet may actually be about 50% pores. Sometimes these spaces are filled with groundwater instead of air.

HANDFUL OF OIL SAND

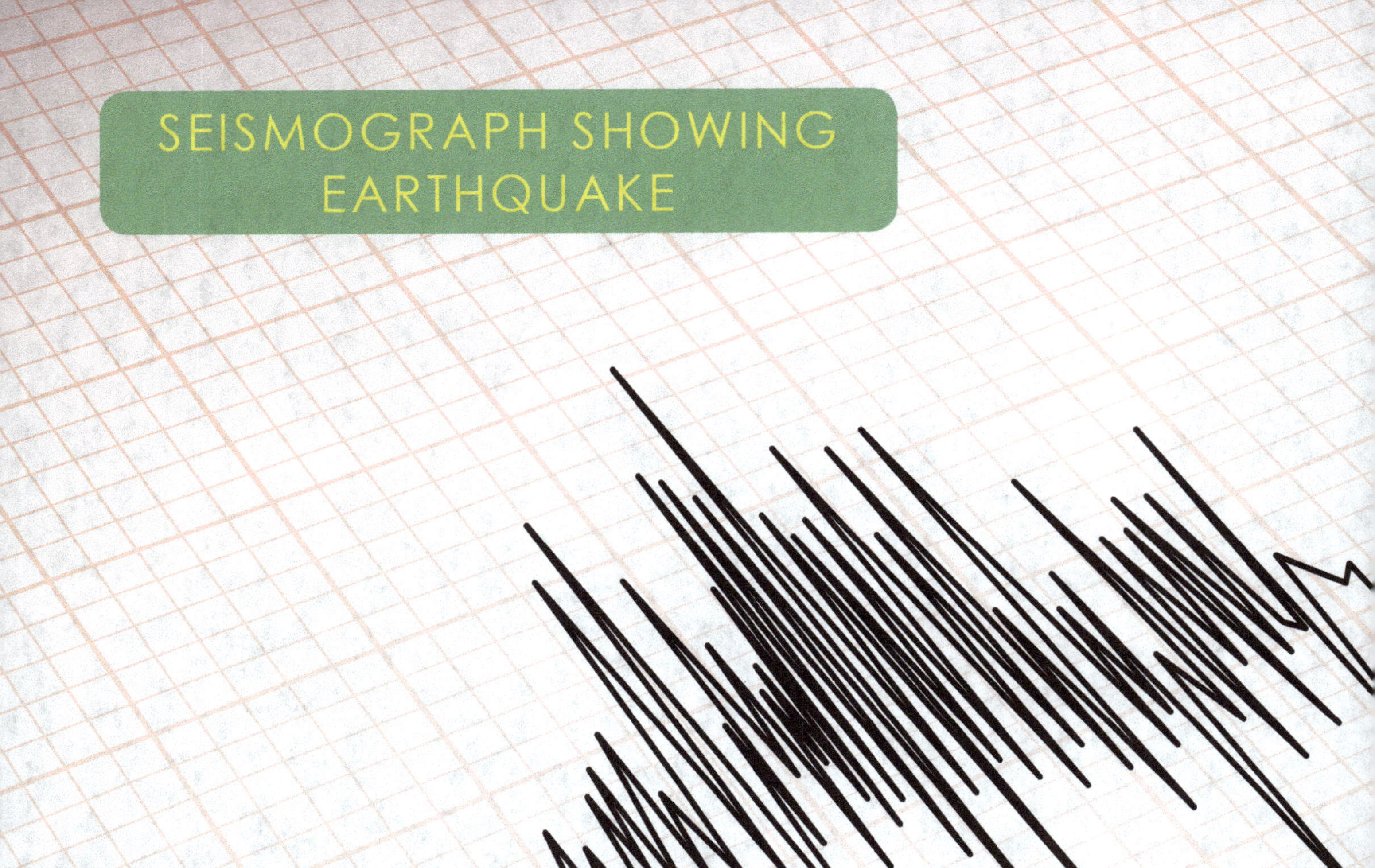
SEISMOGRAPH SHOWING
EARTHQUAKE

When a powerful earthquake travels through land, the seismic waves compress the water and sand in a very short period of time. The water pressure in the moving ground increases dramatically.

Then, the ground gives way because there isn't the needed support and friction between the grains of sand. When the touching of grain to grain is decreased, the sand begins moving like water. This process is liquefaction.

CRACK ON THE GROUND

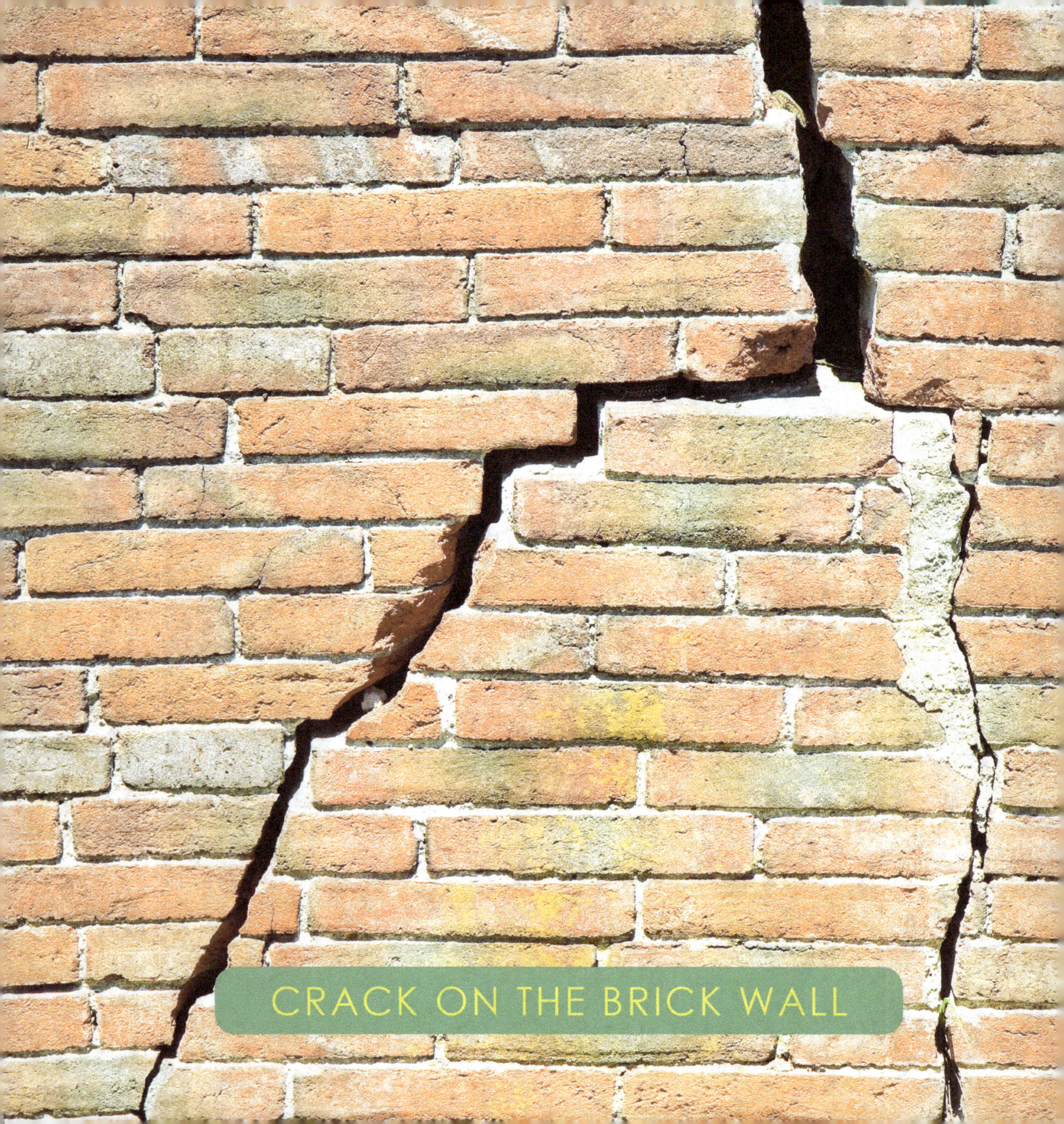

CRACK ON THE BRICK WALL

The brick building almost topples or does come down to the ground because its foundation doesn't have a base of even support anymore. The storage tank comes to the surface, because it's less dense than the sand that surrounds it. It was being held underground by the sand and now the sand is moving like liquid so there's nothing to hold it.

The consequences of liquefaction are devastating, but since a large part of the world's population lives in earthquake territory, engineers and scientists are always researching ways to make buildings more resilient to the threat of earthquakes.

ENGINEERS AT CONTRUCTION SITE

EXPERIMENT 2: PASTA QUAKE

To do this experiment, you'll need at least a 1-pound package of spaghetti. You might need a second box just to be sure you have enough.

NEXT STEPS

Separate the pieces of spaghetti in the box. You should have 1 piece and 32 pieces in two different groups. In the third group, you should have 1000 pieces.

DO THE EXPERIMENT

Hold just one piece of spaghetti in your hands. Push on it and bend it until it breaks. Pay attention to how much work you have to do to break the spaghetti in half. Let's call this amount of work a "5" on the scale for pasta earthquakes.

Now, take the second group of 32 strands of dry spaghetti. Bend this group until it breaks.

Pay attention to how much work you have to do to get this group to break.

It's a lot harder to break than the first group, but you're going to label it a "6" on the scale for pasta earthquakes.

It's time to tackle the last group of 1,000 pieces. Bend this group until you can break them. It's going to take some work! You've now identified the "7" on the scale for pasta earthquakes.

SCIENTIFIC EXPLANATION

In the past, a scale called the Richter scale was used to measure the energy of earthquakes. Today, we use the moment magnitude scale, which is written as MW. This type of scale is an exponential scale, which simply means that each number represents an amount of energy many, many times more powerful than the one that preceded it.

On the moment magnitude scale an increase from 5 to 6 represents an amount of energy that is 32 times larger.

Also, an increase from 5 to 7, a jump of 2 units, actually represents an amount of energy that is 1000 times more powerful.

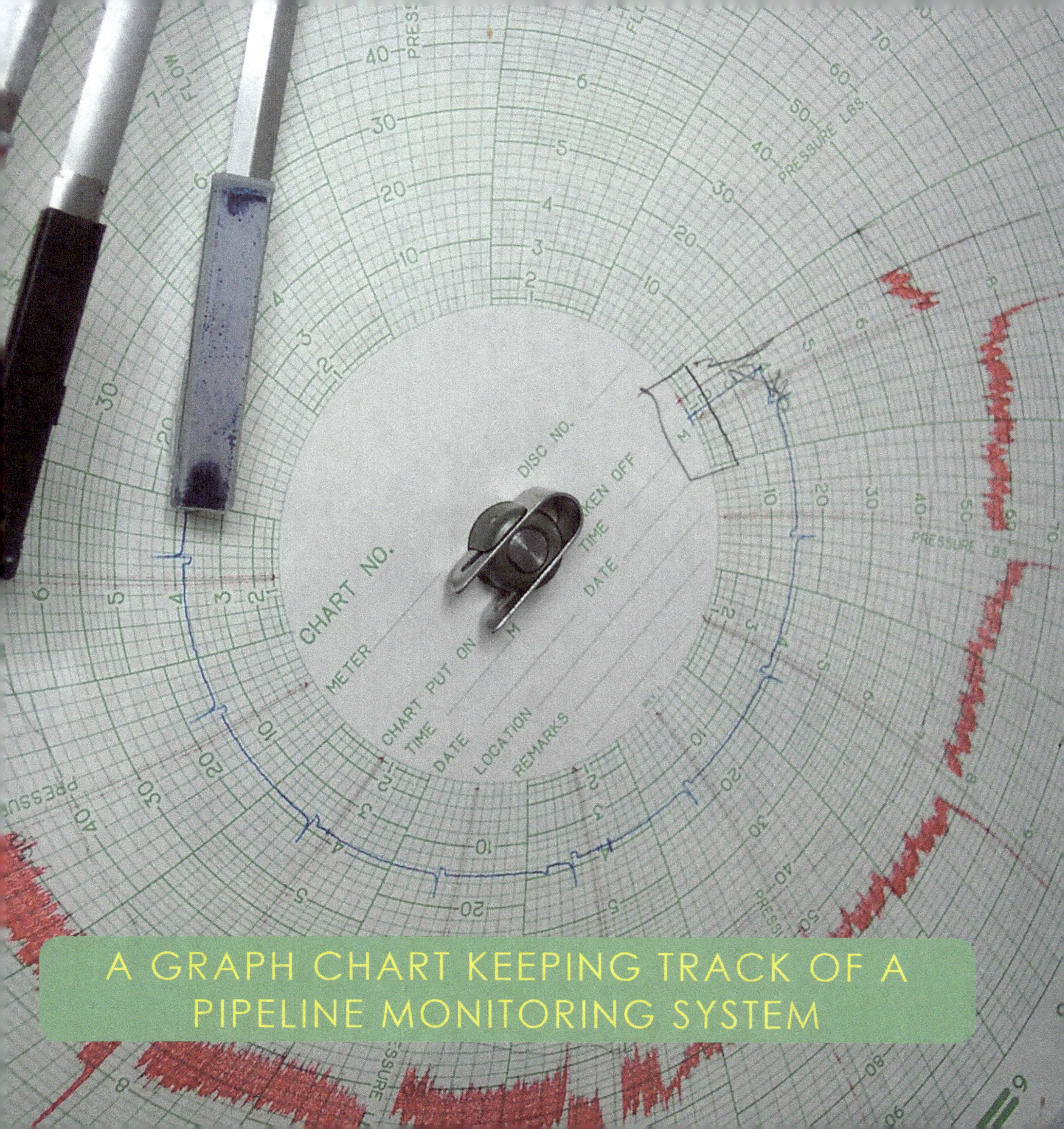

A GRAPH CHART KEEPING TRACK OF A
PIPELINE MONITORING SYSTEM

TSUNAMI WARNING HORN
FOUND ON THE BEACH

This means that if you have an earthquake that measures 7 on this scale, it releases the same amount of energy as 1,000 earthquakes that measure 5 on the scale! This is how your pasta experiment was set up.

An earthquake that measures a 6 on the scale would release the same amount of energy as a small atomic bomb, about 63 terajoules of energy.

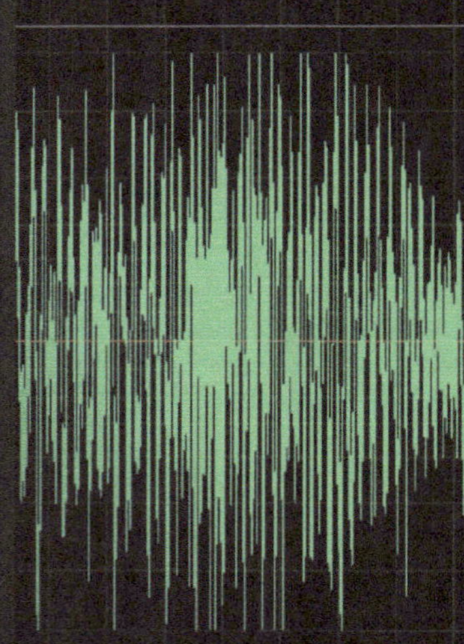

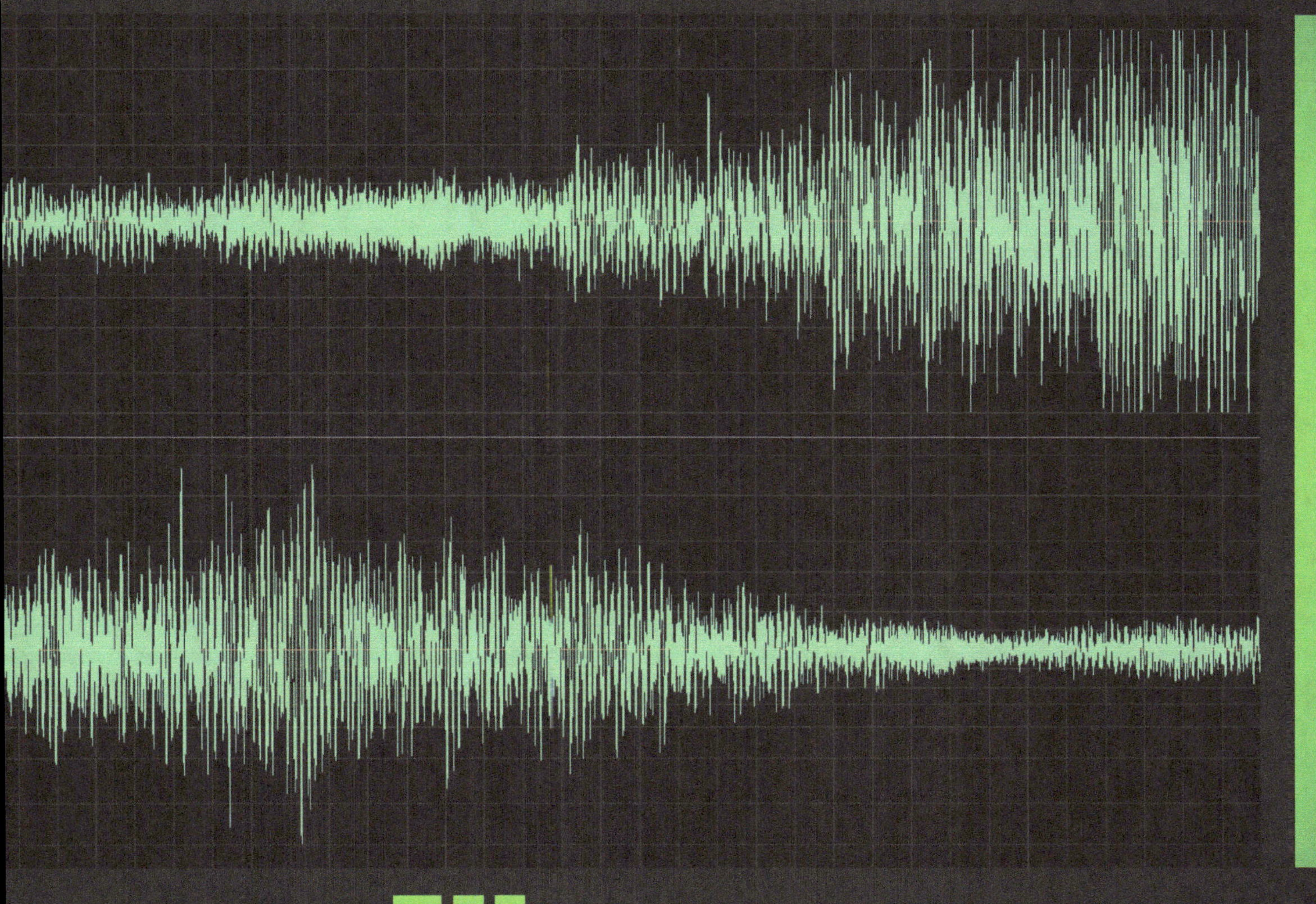

HQUAKE SENSOR
CTIVITY 6.5 RICHTER SCALE

GREAT CHILEAN EARTHQUAKE

The largest earthquake that was recorded in modern times was called the Great Chilean Earthquake. It happened on May 22 in the year 1960 in Southern Chile near Valdivia. The liquefaction from this earthquake damaged and destroyed thousands of buildings.

The government of Chile estimated that over 2 million people were made homeless. Prior to the larger earthquake, the day before, there was a powerful series of foreshocks of magnitude 7.9. The tsunamis created from the earthquake had waves that were over 80 feet tall.

AFTERMATH OF THE 1960 CHILEAN
TSUNAMI IN HILO, HAWAI'I

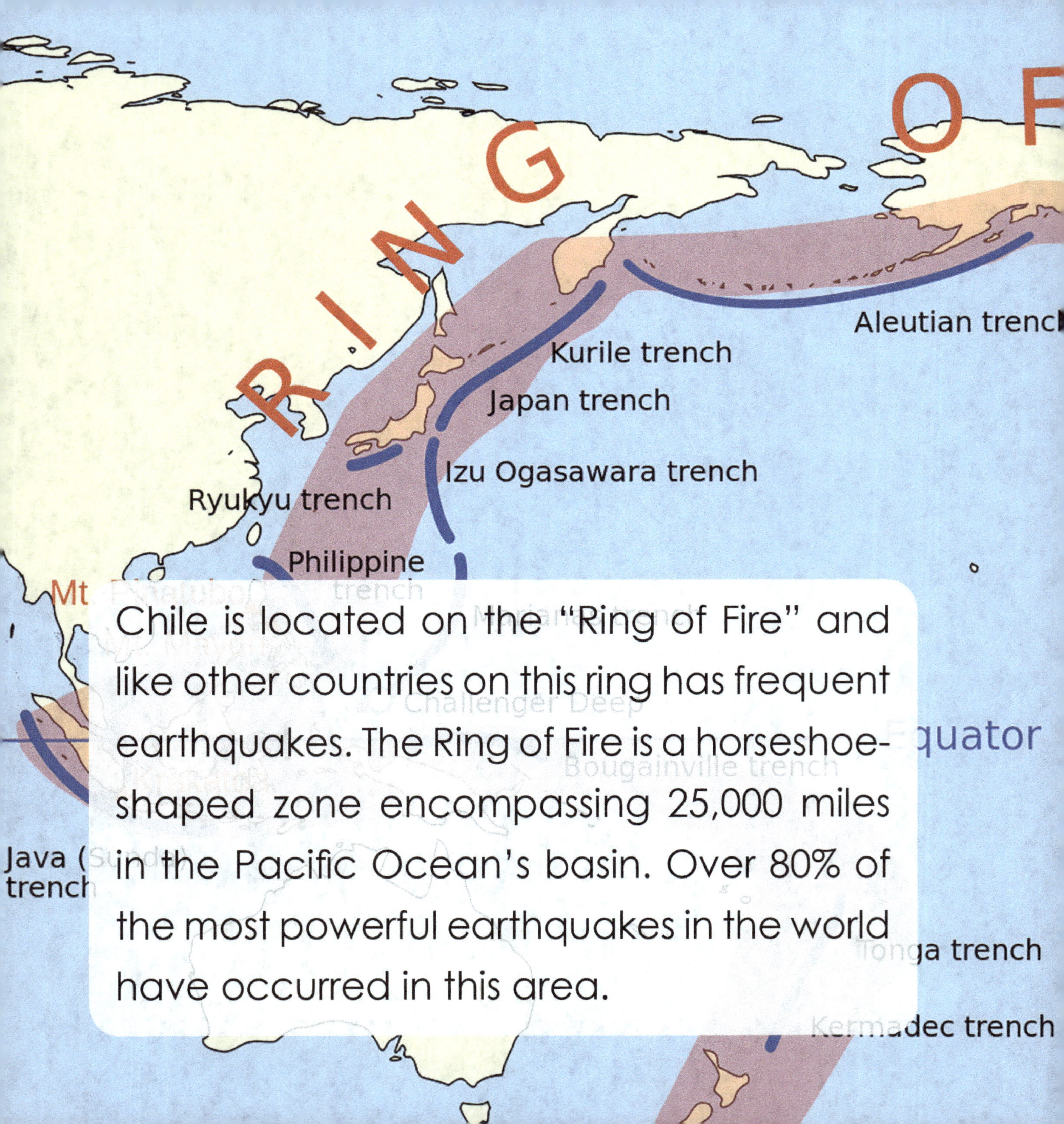

Chile is located on the "Ring of Fire" and like other countries on this ring has frequent earthquakes. The Ring of Fire is a horseshoe-shaped zone encompassing 25,000 miles in the Pacific Ocean's basin. Over 80% of the most powerful earthquakes in the world have occurred in this area.

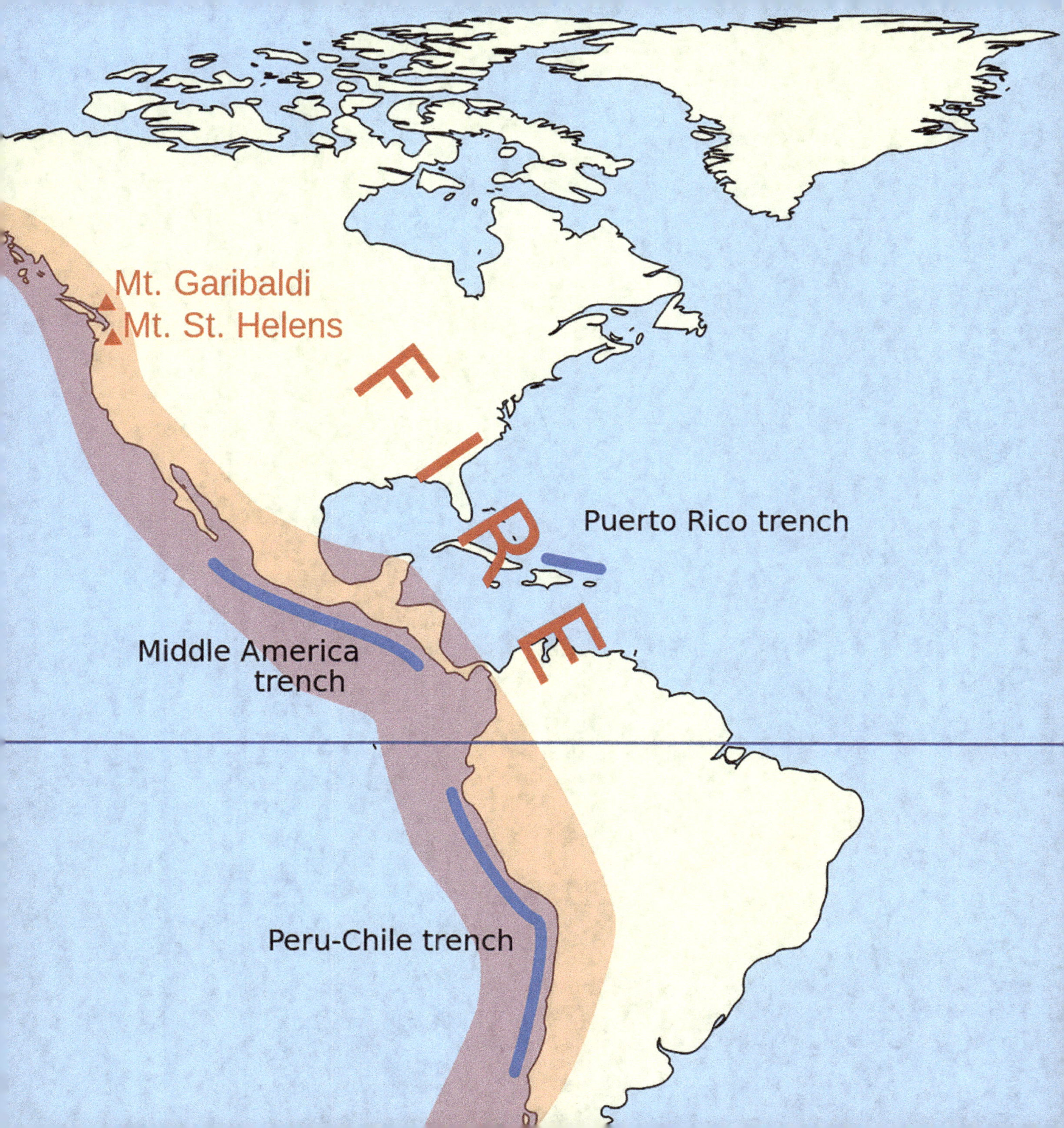

Mt. Garibaldi
Mt. St. Helens
FIRE
Puerto Rico trench
Middle America trench
Peru-Chile trench

Most of the Earth's volcanoes are located here as well, because this is where the most subduction zones are. These zones are places where one tectonic plate is shoved underneath another tectonic plate.

A SCENIC VIEW OF MAYON
VOLCANO, PHILIPPINES

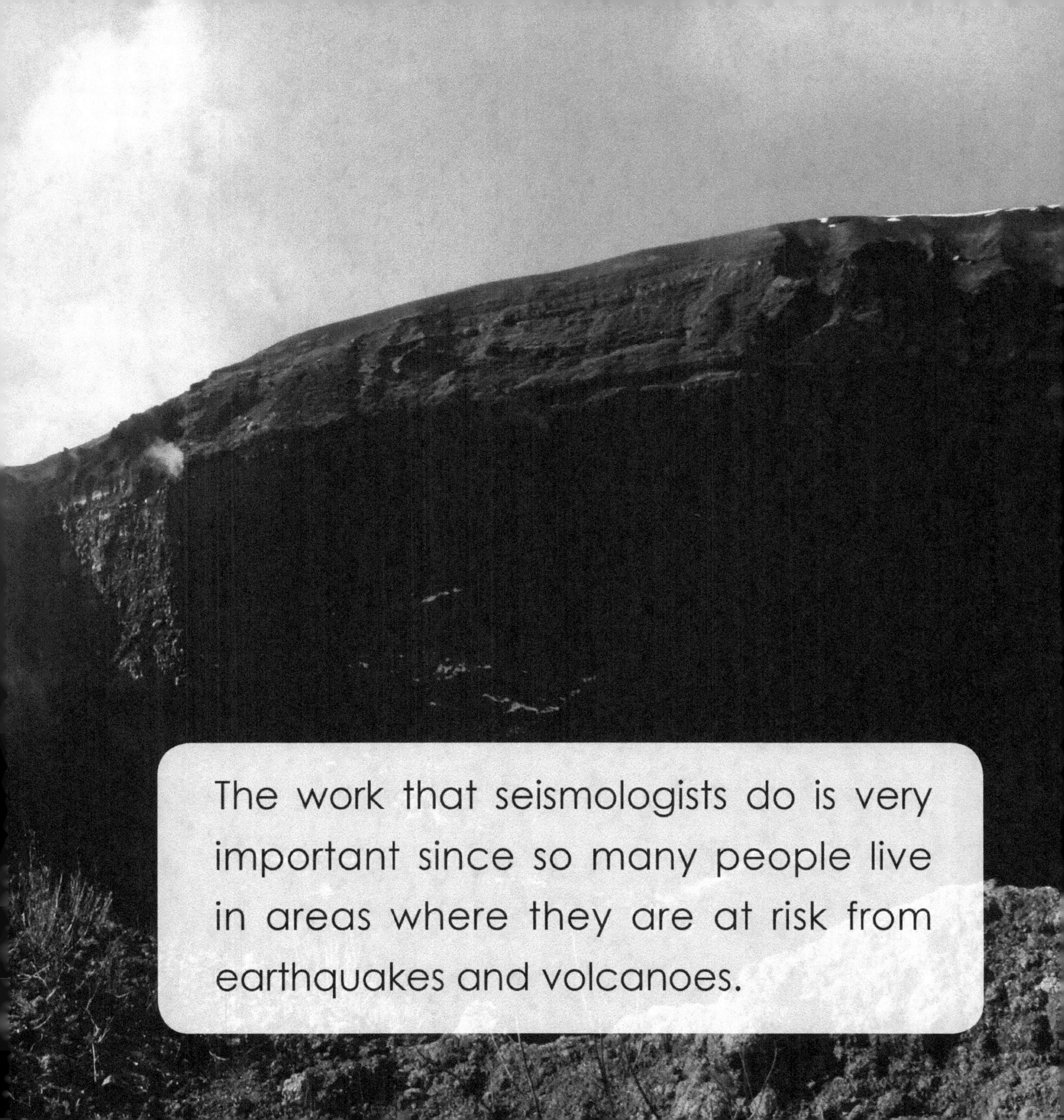

The work that seismologists do is very important since so many people live in areas where they are at risk from earthquakes and volcanoes.

Now you know more about Earth Science by doing your own experiments. You can find more Science Education books from Baby Professor by searching the website of your favorite book retailer.

Visit

BABY PROFESSOR
EDUCATION KIDS

www.BabyProfessorBooks.com
to download Free Baby Professor eBooks
and view our catalog of new and exciting
Children's Books